SWINGALONG SONGS
by Sue Stevens

with piano accompaniments
by Geoffry Russell-Smith

Cover designed by Carole Logan

THE GREATEST MUSIC COMPANY IN THE WORLD

ISBN 0 86175 228 7

CONTENTS

GUITAR CHORDS Please note these do not always conform exactly to the harmony of the piano part.

THE WORLD KEEPS TURNING AROUND

Sue Stevens

With a swinging 2 in a bar

VERSE

1 We all live in the big wide world As the world keeps turn-ing a round, —

We all live in the big wide world As the world keeps turn-ing a - round, —

4

2 North and South and East and West,
   Still the world keeps turning around. *(three times)*
   As the big wide world keeps turning around.

3 Upside down or the right way up,
   Still the world keeps turning around.
   As the big wide world keeps turning around.

4 Make a new friend ev'ry day
   As the world keeps turning around.
   As the big wide world keeps turning around.

Make up verses of your own to suit your school or club.

SING-ALONG SONG

Sue Stevens

*   The leader to improvise alternatives, e.g., whistling, nonsense words,
    clapping etc., varying it for each time round.

THE SKELETON STOMP

Sue Stevens

Stealthily, but not too slow

All in the mid-dle of the night!

All in the mid-dle of the night! Squeaks and groans and— rat-tl - ing bones,

All in the mid-dle of the night! Come to the ske-le-tons' par - ty,

❋ Different percussion effects could be improvised for each verse.

Come to the ske-le-tons' romp: 1 See that ghoul____ play-ing the fool,

D   Em   F#m   F#7   Bm   A7   D   Em

D.C.

Do - ing the ske - le - ton stomp.

C#7   F#7   Bm

(The following lines to be added cumulatively on each repeat in the bars marked ❋ ❋)

2 See that cat in a pink top hat,

3 See that elf enjoying himself,

4 See that frog jiggle and jog,

5 See that toad from down the road,

6 See that ghost munching toast,

7 See that spider full of cider,

8 See that snake shimmy and shake,

9 See that witch from out of the ditch,

SI, SI, SI

Traditional Congolese

Gently, at beguine tempo

Si, si, si, si, do-la-da, Ya-cu si-ne-la-du, ba-na-ha. Si, si, si, si, do-la-da, Ya-cu

SOMETIME, SOMEWHERE

Sue Stevens

2   Where the breakers wash the shore
    And the sea is deep and blue;
    Where the mewing seagulls soar
    And the sands are ever-new:

3   Where the fields are fresh and green
    And the hedgerow sweet with briar;
    Where the hawthorns gently lean
    And the stream is shot with fire:

4   Where a silence fills the night
    And the moon hangs in the sky;
    Where the stars are diamond-bright
    And the clouds go drifting by:

✻ Optional second part.

SATURDAY SONG

Sue Stevens

2 Rivers are just the place
   With a rod and a line—
   Having a picnic lunch
   When the weather's fine: *Chorus*

3 Kicking a ball around
   In the city park,
   Covered in lovely mud—
   Won't go home 'til dark:

4 Meeting another gang
   When we're on the bus,
   We don't think much of them—
   They don't care for us:

MOVING ON

Sue Stevens

geese fly in-to the sun-rise I'll be gone. 1 There is dust up-on my hands, There is dust up-on my feet; It's time for me to be mov-ing on. _____ There is dust up-on the fac-es of the peo-ple that I meet: It's time for me to be mov-ing on. Mov-ing on, mov-ing on. _____

2   They laid bricks around my feet,
    They laid bricks around my head;
    It's time for me to be moving on—
    They laid bricks until the sky had gone
    And all the grass was dead:
    It's time for me to be moving on.

3   There are mountains to be climbed,
    There are oceans to be sailed;
    It's time for me to be moving on—
    There are rivers to be followed,
    There are forests to be trailed:
    It's time for me to be moving on.

THE DINOSAUR SONG

Sue Stevens

now there are none,— Their time was up— and they had to move on.——
now there are none,— Their time was up— and they had to move on.——

Bb   C7   C7   F

CHORUS

So when your time is up— you've got to move a-long, When your time is up— you've

F   C7   C7

got to move a-long. You can't stop the clock:— it still keeps tick-ing on! You've

F   F7   Bb

1,2,3   **4**

got to move on — when your time is gone.—   time is gone.—

F   (G7)   C7   F   C7   F   sfz

3 Where, O where have the pirate kings gone?
Where, O where have the pirate kings gone?
They all walked the plank, and now there are none,
Their time was up and they had to move on.

4 Where, O where have the sorcerers gone?
Where, O where have the sorcerers gone?
'Twas "Abracadabra!" and now there are none,
Their time was up and they had to move on.

COME TO THE FAIR!

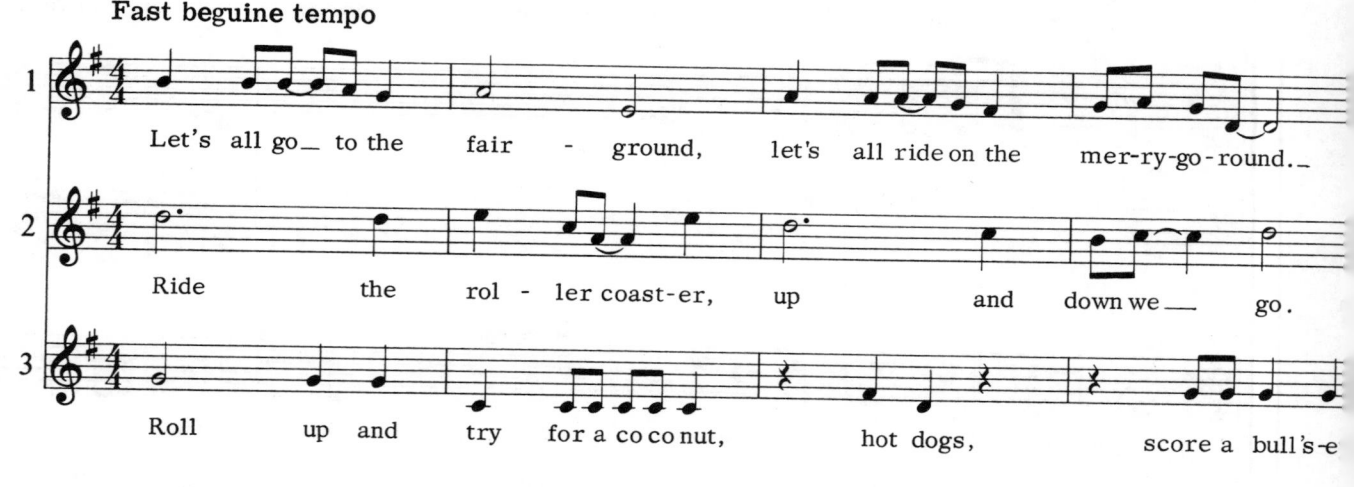

Fast beguine tempo

1. Let's all go— to the fair - ground, let's all ride on the mer-ry-go-round.—

2. Ride the rol - ler coast-er, up and down we— go.

3. Roll up and try for a co co nut, hot dogs, score a bull's-e

G C D7 G

DUBI DU

1. Du - bi du - bi du, du - bi du,— du - bi du-bi du, du - bi du.—

2. Du - bi du - bi du, du - bi du,— du - bi du -bi du, du - bi du.—

3. Du-bi du, du-bi du, du-bi du du-bi du

4. Du - bi du, du-bi du, du - bi du, du-bi du

* The keyboard accompaniment may be used to accompany both rounds.

Sue Stevens

ad and round on the big wheel, let's all go_ to the fair!

ie and bring your friends,_ for ev' - ry-bo - dy is there.

- fee-ap - ples and pri - zes for ev'ry-one, come to the fair!

Am   D7   G

Sue Stevens

- bi du - bi du, du - bi du,_ du - bi du - bi du du.

- bi du - bi du, du - bi du,_ du - bi du - bi du du.

du - bi du, du - bi du, du - bi du du.

- bi du, du - bi du, du - du - bi du du.

THE CUCKOO CLOCK

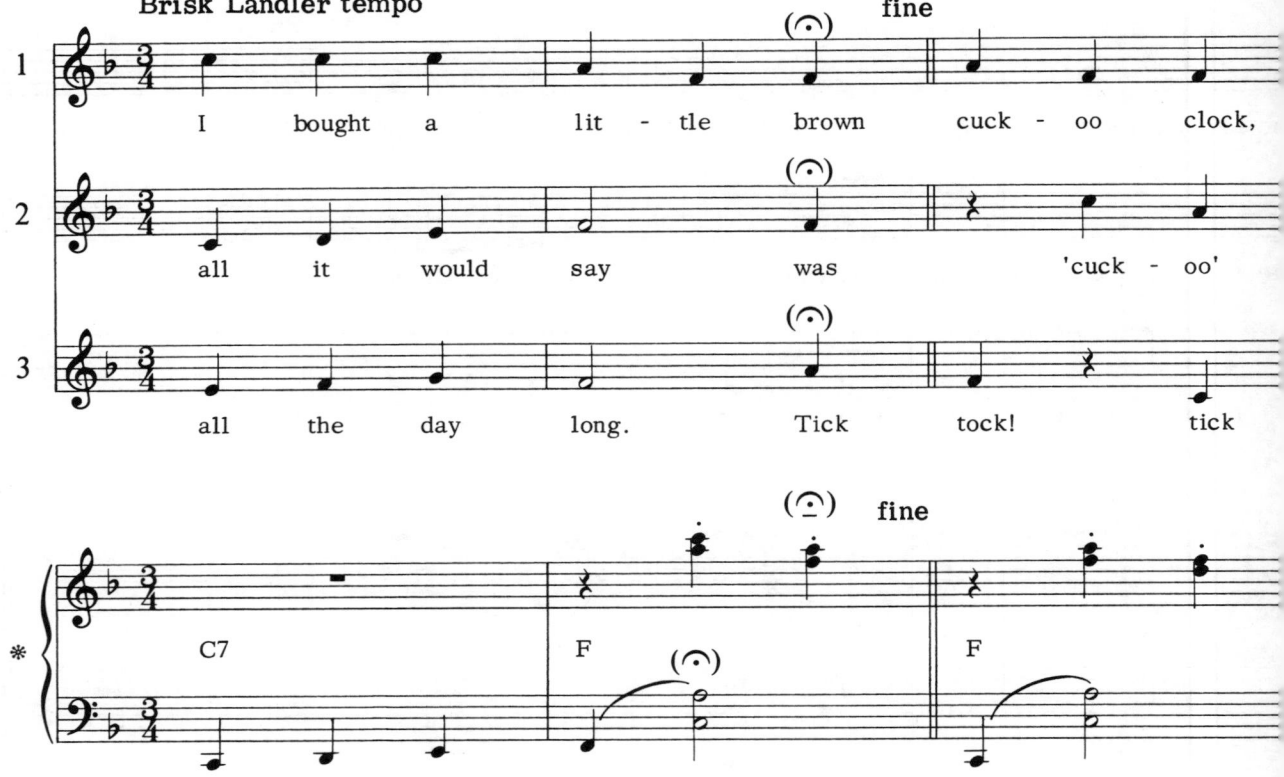

THE WEATHER FORECAST

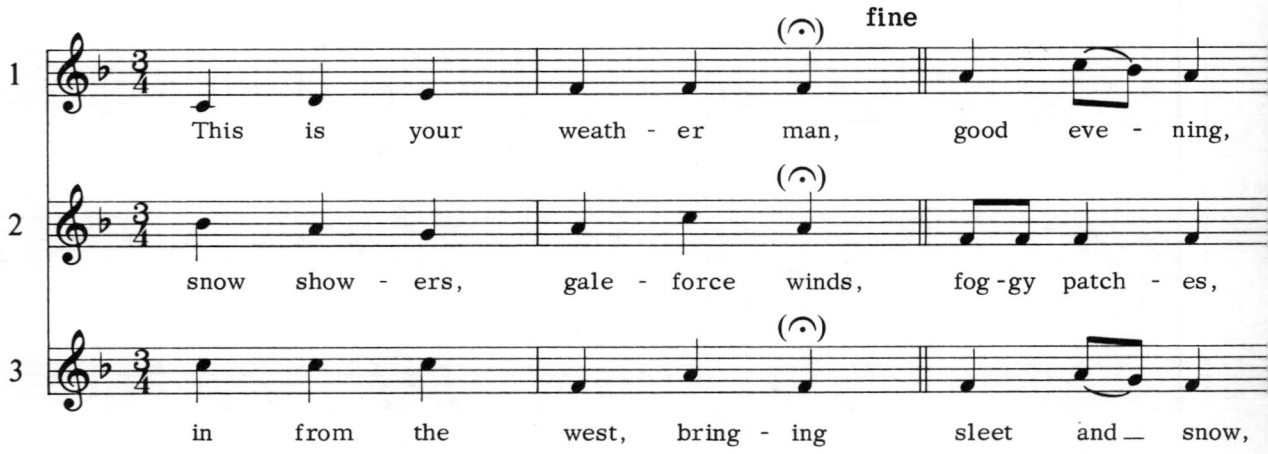

* The keyboard accompaniment may be used to accompany both rounds.

Sue Stevens

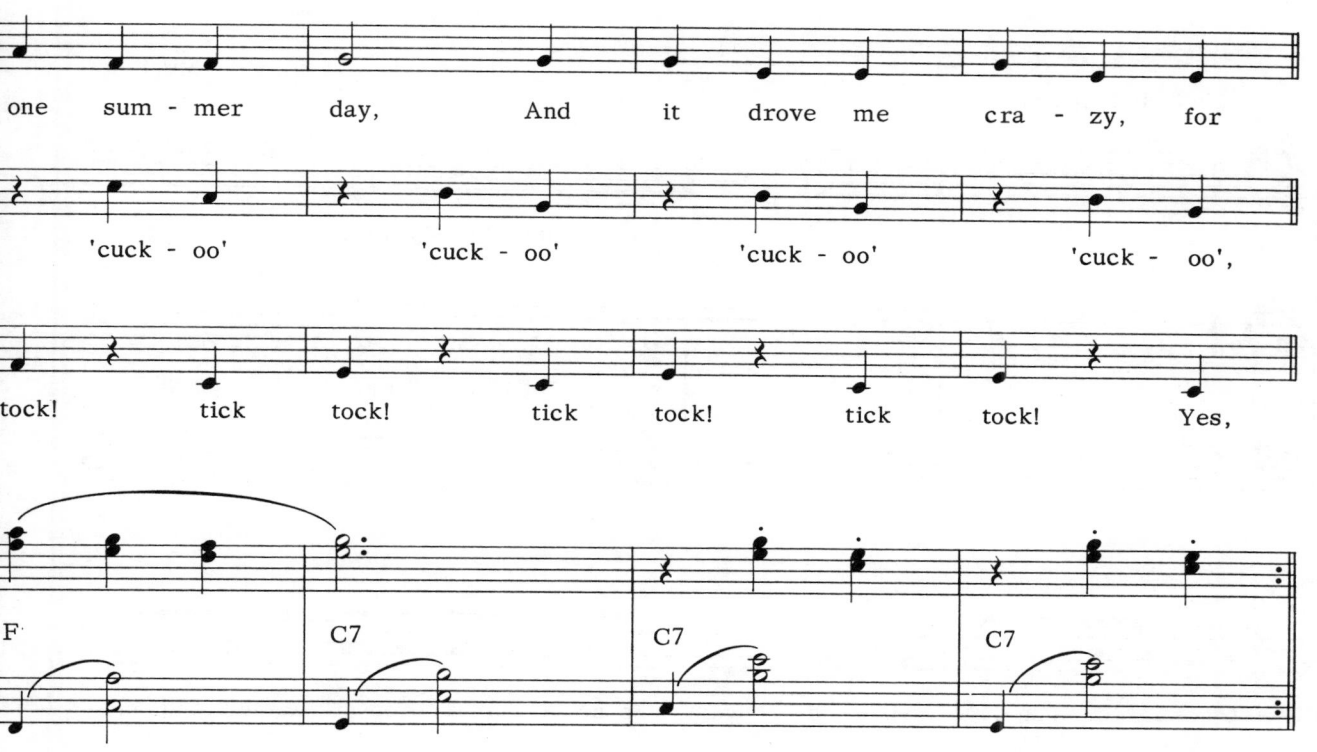

one sum - mer day, And it drove me cra - zy, for

'cuck - oo' 'cuck - oo' 'cuck - oo' 'cuck - oo',

tock! tick tock! tick tock! tick tock! Yes,

F   C7   C7   C7

Sue Stevens

here is the weath-er fore - cast, there will be bright in-ter-vals,

vi - si - bil - i - ty al - most nil, thun - der storms spread-ing

is your jour - ney nec-es-sa - ry? Bet-ter stay at home!

DESE BONES A-GONNA RISE AGAIN

Spiritual

2   He took a rib from Adam's side *
    Made Miss Eve to be his bride.

3   Put them in a garden rich and fair,
    Told them to eat what they found there.

4   To one tall tree they must not go—
    There must the fruit for ever grow.

5   Miss Eve she came a-walking 'round,
    Spied that tree all laden down.

6   Serpent he came 'round the trunk;
    At Miss Eve his eye he wunk.

7   First she took a little pull,
    Then she filled her apron full.

8   Adam he came prowling 'round,
    Spied them peelings on the ground.

9   Then he took a little slice;
    Smacked his lips and said "How nice!"

10 The Lord then rose up in His wrath,
    Told them to "beat it down the path."

11 He said to Adam "Dis de end!
    You no longer is my friend."

✳   *Dese bones a-gonna rise again*   after each line.

POOR ADAM

Traditional American

2 And he never had no childhood
Playing 'round the cabin door,
And he never had a mammy
For to lift him off the floor.

3 And he never had a pappy
For to tell him all he knowed,
And he never had a mammy
To point out the narrow road.

4 And he never had that feeling,
When at night he went to rest,
Of a possum sweet potato
Tucked away inside his vest.

5 And I've always had a feeling
He'd a let that apple be
If he'd only had a mammy
For to rock him on her knee.

TAILS, TAILS, TAILS

Sue Stevens

thump on wood-en floors, Or p'raps a warm and fluf-fy one to curl a - round your

B7   Gm   D   Cdim   Em

CHORUS

paws? _____ Tails, tails, tails, you can swing them to and fro, You can

A7   D   Em   A7

wrap them round your mid-dle, You can trail them in the snow, You can

D   Em   A7

wave them when you're an - gry, You can wag them when you're glad, You can

D   F#7   B7   Gm

optional repeat

chase them
round and } round and round and round and round and round and round and round and round and round and round and round and round un-til you drive _____ the neigh-bours mad.

mad.

2 And would you like it stripey, speckled, plain or maybe spotted?
   And would you wear it curly, straight or elegantly knotted?
   And if it were prehensile, what enormous fun to be
   The envy of the neighbours as you swung from tree to tree!

3 If tails were made detachable, how useful it would be
   To change your tail for parties, or for going to the sea;
   Or, if you're going out at night, with safety first in mind,
   To wear a red fluorescent one to light you up behind!

TUMBALALAIKA

Traditional Yiddish

2 Maiden, maiden can you explain:
   What can grow, yet never needs rain?
   Which is the fire that burns through the years?
   Which is the sorrow deeper than tears?

3 Listen, listen while I reply:
   A stone can grow, and always be dry;
   Love that is true will burn through the years;
   When a heart cries, it cries without tears.

THE COCONUT TREE

Sue Stevens

ONE DAY

Sue Stevens

YELLOW BIRD

Traditional Jamaican

JUGGERNAUT JOE

Sue Stevens

2 And I bought him a little tin flute
   And he danced to and fro _____ (etc.)

3 And I bought him a shiny top hat
   Which he wore just for show __

4 And I bought him some wellington boots
   To wear in rain and snow _____

5 And I bought him a satchel and books
   So off to school he'd go _____

Plus any you care to make up.

Printed in Great Britain by Hobbs the Printers of Southampton 5/86